Don't Do That, Dexter!

WRITTEN BY JODEE MCCONNAUGHHAY

ILLUSTRATED BY RICHARD MAX KOLDING

ISBN 0-7847-1690-0

11 10 09 08 07 06   9 8 7 6 5 4 3 2

Standard®
PUBLISHING
Bringing The Word to Life
Cincinnati, Ohio

Running, jumping, through the house,
seems like fun, you see.

But Mommy says, "Don't do that, Dexter!
Outside's the place to be."

Running, jumping, through the house,
I slipped and skinned my knee.
Mommy washed and bandaged it,
and kissed me on the cheek.

*Obey your parents in the Lord, for
this is right!*

Driving, dumping, digging deep,
I make trucks bump and roar.
Then Daddy said,
"It's time for a snack—
when your trucks are off the floor."

Driving, dumping, digging deep,
I bumped and roared some more.
Then Mommy said, "No snack tonight—
I see trucks still on the floor."

Obey your parents in the Lord,
for this is right!

Swinging on the curtains,

a super hero—*whee!*

'Til Daddy said, "Now that's enough.

It's time to go to sleep."

Swinging on the curtains
caused such a mess for Dad.
When they crumpled to the floor,
it really made him sad.

Obey your parents in the Lord,
for this is right!

Bouncing on my bed at night,
a spaceman on the moon.
But Daddy says this astronaut
should settle down real soon.

Bouncing on my bed at night,
I bounced right off the bed.
I cried and cried and Daddy came
with ice for my bumped head.

Obey your parents in the Lord,
for this is right!

You don't have to tell me twice;

I'm as smart as I can be.

When Mom and Dad say,

"Don't do that!"

It's because they love me!

Children, obey your parents in the Lord,
for this is right. —Ephesians 6:1